SOCIETY AND THE VICTORIANS
LITERATURE AT NURSE

LITERATURE AT NURSE, OR CIRCULATING MORALS:

A Polemic on Victorian Censorship

George Moore

Edited with an introduction by
PIERRE COUSTILLAS
Director, Centre for Victorian Studies,
University of Lille

THE HARVESTER PRESS
HUMANITIES PRESS

This edition first published in 1976 by
THE HARVESTER PRESS LIMITED
Publisher: John Spiers
2 Stanford Terrace, Hassocks,
Sussex, England
and in the USA by
Humanities Press Inc.,
Atlantic Highlands, NJ 07716

Literature at Nurse
first published in 1885 by Henry Vizetelly, London

The Harvester Press Limited
British Library Cataloguing in Publication Data
Moore, George
Literature at nurse. – [1st ed. reprinted].
(Society and the Victorians; no. 29)
ISBN 0-85527-164-7
1. Title 2. Series
025.2'1 Z675.S8
Libraries, Subscription
Libraries – Great Britain – Censorship
English fiction – History and criticism

Humanities Press Inc
Library of Congress Cataloging in Publication Data
Moore, George, 1852–1933.
Literature at nurse.
(Society and the Victorians; no. 29)
1. Libraries, Rental – Great Britain. – History.
2. Censorship – Great Britain – History. 3. English fiction – 19th century – History and criticism.
4. Publishers and publishing – Great Britain – History.
I. Title. II. Series.
Z791:A1M57 1976 070.5'73'0941 76–6138
ISBN 0–391–00588–X

Printed in Great Britain by Biddles Ltd., Guildford, Surrey

Contents

PART ONE

Introduction

by Pierre Coustillas

Introduction

Any artistic achievement rests on the combination of personal and impersonal factors – of individual talent or genius and of the material and cultural climate prevailing at the time. Modes and conventions either attract or repel; they rarely leave one indifferent. The artist may well try to please himself first, he may indeed indulge in the thought that he makes no concession to the times, yet the passing of the years invariably throws into relief those elements of his work which are a reflection of contemporary realities. Naturally, this is patent when strong external influences mould a work of art. Where the novel is concerned the mode of publication or distribution has a notable effect, not only on its sale, but also on its contents, if the writer seeks to satisfy the demands of the market. Of this the publication of fiction in the nineteenth century offers a striking example – striking to the point of being ludicrous to the uninitiated foreign observer. The average Continental reader is always puzzled and/or amused to hear that English novels under Victoria were as a rule published in three volumes. The notion seems exceedingly odd. Yet the English did publish their novels in three-volume form with perverse obstinacy for the most part of the nineteenth century, and the cultured classes largely looked on this as a matter of course.

The present pamphlet, written by George Moore in 1885, is a spirited attack on this idiosyncratic system, and both its import and its impact, if they are to be gauged correctly, must be seen in the light of a situation which came abruptly to an end some ten years later. It is essentially an onslaught on circulating libraries and the proprietor of the largest of these, Charles Edward Mudie, who came – not altogether unfairly – to be identified with the three-volume system and its moral censorship of literature. Traditionally English fiction had been issued in multi-volume form, but Walter Scott having published his novels with great success in three volumes, it practically became the rule for authors to publish their works of fiction in this format. There were of course exceptions – officially stories in one volume were never banned, and some occasionally achieved publication in two or even four volumes. The price of a three-volume set was high –

one guinea and a half, that is more than a working man would usually earn in a week – and here again the influence of Scott was decisive. *Waverley,* his first novel in that form, was only priced at a guinea; *Kenilworth* (1821) established the price that was to remain statutory until the three-decker collapsed at the turn of the century. A guinea and a half was only nominally the price, for, indeed, very few individuals could afford to purchase fiction that was so expensive, and circulating libraries obtained copies with a substantial discount. Mudie's Select Library and its rival, W. H. Smith's, ruled the roost, but there were also a number of minor libraries with branches scattered throughout Britain. As they were practically the only buyers of novels issued at 31s. 6d per set they came to exercise a strong influence which amounted to a virtual monopoly. The annual subscription of one guinea for any three volumes at a time was low in comparison with the rates offered by other libraries early in the Victorian age, yet it excluded lower-class people who could read fluently. At a time when free public libraries were still few and were developing but slowly, Mudie and Smith encouraged the publication of novels in three volumes essentially because they thrived on it; similarly, they looked down upon novels issued more practically in one volume. For the average novelist of no particular merit who tried to make a living out of fiction, it was clearly an advantage to write long novels that could be brought out as three-deckers, since publishers could offer more for such novels, selling at 18s. or 15s. to the libraries than for a one-volume story priced at 6s. in the bookshops, but sold with a 2s. discount to booksellers. But the system, as has been noted time and again, was to have consequences no one had foreseen – the circulating libraries gradually exerted a material, intellectual and moral dictatorship on authors, publishers and readers.

On authors, because they had to gratify the tastes of a strictly circumscribed class of readers, whose response to the first edition conditioned the book's subsequent publishing history. The reception of the first edition (which, as often as not, was limited to 500 copies) worked as a tester – a publisher who had done badly with the three-decker issue would not readily incur the expense of resetting the text for a one-volume edition which must enjoy a sale of several thousand copies if it was to pay its way. (Or at least the publisher was in a favourable position to impose unattractive terms on the author.) It is obvious that the circulating libraries, Mudie's *primus inter pares,* could have a decisive influence on the fate of a book, a situation all the more objectionable because the results of publication in the three-decker format were not a fair test of the literary value of a novel. Nor was the system fair to the reading public at large, who were practically denied access to those stories which, not necessarily for artistic reasons, never went beyond the three-volume stage. The nature of the novels which the general public were given to read was conditioned to a large extent by the taste of the subscribers to circulating libraries. And as three-volume fiction found a notable portion of its readers among the idle females of the middle-classes whose view of life was narrow, the artist's freedom in the choice and treatment of his subject thus was severely restricted. The novel as a genre suffered from this. Not only did the circulating libraries – through the publishers – impose a format which was an absurdity, but they posed as intellectual and moral censors. Mudie and some also publishers (like Bentley, who was no less conventional) became an arbiter of literary taste with the doubtful qualification of a moralising tradesman all too prone to lend an ear to Mrs. Grundy.

George Moore was fully aware of all this and he chafed at Mudie's rule over English fiction. In view of the fact that in after-years he tended to magnify his own role in the decline and fall of the three-decker, it must be realized that he was not first in the field. Among his predecessors was James Thomson, the poet of *The City of Dreadful Night,* who in 1865 inveighed against the spirit of Bumble and the subservience of contemporary literature to it. Similarly Matthew Arnold, writing in the *Fortnightly Review* in March 1880, observed that 'as our nation grows more civilised, as a real love of reading comes to prevail more widely, the system which keeps up the present exorbitant price of new books in England, the system of lending-libraries from which books are hired, will be seen to be, as it is, eccentric, artificial, and unsatisfactory in the highest degree. It is a machinery for the multiplication and protection of bad literature, and for keeping good books dear.' There is no doubt that by discouraging English people from buying new fiction, and indeed new books, the circulating libraries played an anti-social role, and that by enforcing an arbitrary format they did English fiction a great disservice. They also tended to deprive it of its potential originality: dullness and conventionality came to be recognised as the distinctive features of the circulating-library novel. Controversial subjects of an ideological nature had to be avoided by novelists lest they should shock the middle-class female readers, the typical young lady of the period and her strait-laced mamma, while on the other hand vapid subjects treated in a sensational or sentimental manner were systematically cultivated by novelists who sought library patronage. These points had been made many times, in public or in private, by many writers and critics before George Moore. In her excellent book on *Mudie's Circulating Library,* Guinevere Griest quotes a number of anonymous statements in the *Times* and the *Saturday Review* castigating the tyranny of the circulating libraries; such statements distinctly show that the opponents of the libraries were not at a loss for arguments – material, literary, commercial, even social. Thus in 1854 a writer in the *Times* aired the following argument (not quoted by Guinevere Griest) which one would more readily have expected to find in, say, Bradlaugh's *National Reformer:* 'We simply ask, on behalf of all classes, but especially in the interest of the masses of the people, that the old and vicious method of proceeding shall be reversed – that, instead of commencing with editions of a guinea, and gradually coming down in the course of years to cheap editions of 5s., all good books on their first appearance shall appeal to the needy multitude, while the requirements of the fortunate and lazier few are postponed to a more convenient season.' Publication in cheap weekly or monthly parts went some way to meet this demand; indeed Dickens and some other popular novelists availed themselves of it with great success, but by the 1870s it had ceased to be a challenge to the three-volume novel. On the other hand, the various attempts made by publishers to bring out original editions of novels at low prices had failed to tempt book buyers as opposed to book borrowers. The circulating libraries, when Moore started on his career, were still all-powerful. They would not hear of one-volume fiction – an open threat to their monopoly – and they knew that the banishment of a three-decker from their genteel shelves sealed its fate. Meredith's *The Ordeal of Richard Feverel* is a case in point.

George Moore's first novel, *A Modern Lover,* appeared in the early summer of 1883 in the 'statutory' three-volume form. It was a realistic novel dealing with the adventures of a young artist in London which Tinsley, a timid publisher of the old school, had agreed to publish on condition that Moore should pay him whatever difference there was between the production cost and the proceeds from the sales to circulating libraries. In his story Moore stood revealed on every page as an imitator of French naturalistic fiction. The hero, Lewis Seymour, is an English version of Maupassant's Georges Duroy in *Bel Ami,* though chronology rules out the suggestion of influence. Among the three girls whom he seduces and exploits is one Gwynnie Lloyd, a Bible-reading, lower-class girl, who poses *in puris naturalibus* to save him from the river. The British press, as Moore recorded with self-satisfaction, welcomed the story, but Mudie, who only bought 50 copies of the book, refused to circulate them after two ladies from the country had objected to the scene in which Gwynnie Lloyd sits to Seymour as a model for Venus. Now an Irishman usually loves a fight, and Moore forthwith entered the fray. Luck assisted him in several ways. He owed Tinsley £40, but a providential fire at the publisher's disposed of the copies of the novel that remained unsold and it was Tinsley's insurer, not Moore, who recouped him for his losses. Moore also found a paper, the *Pall Mall Gazette,* that was prepared to accept an article about the treatment he suffered at the hands of Mudie, and to publish it prominently. Lastly, he succeeded in persuading a sympathetic publisher, Henry Vizetelly, to take his next book, *A Mummer's Wife.*

Moore's attack on the circulating libraries in his early career was two-pronged. First, he wrote the article reprinted here entitled 'A New Censorship of Literature', which appeared in the *Pall Mall Gazette,* an evening newspaper of radical tendency when previously under John Morley's editorship and still enjoying this reputation in 1884. The article was printed in the issue for 10 December, 1884, and was followed by some interesting correspondence. The whole material is reprinted here for the first time. The second outburst occurred when Moore had realized that Mudie, whom he had been content to designate as Mr X in the *Pall Mall* article, had blacklisted his second novel, *A Mummer's Wife,* doubtless as a single-volume story which did not bring grist to his mill, but chiefly on account of its so-called immorality. Mr. Mudie, the self-appointed guardian of public virtue, could not put up with the passage in which Dick Lennox, the manager of an opera bouffe company, drags a draper's wife into a room one night and shuts the door. Moore's second attack, cleverly entitled *Literature at Nurse, or Circulating Morals,* appeared in the summer of 1885. This three-penny pamphlet issued under Vizetelly's imprint is also reprinted here for the first time; it has become so scarce that when a copy turns up in a sale-room, it is likely to fetch several hundred pounds. The cool reception it met may be attributed to a variety of causes: its brash, cocksure tone must have caused not a few critics to recoil; it was ostensibly a plea *pro domo sua,* and, if one leaves aside the question of realism and morality, it amounted to an apology for and a boosting of novels – his own *Modern Lover* and *Mummer's Wife* – which did not belong to the pick of literature. Typical was the reaction of the *Academy* in August 1885: 'His argument that [the] censorship [of fiction] has not been exercised with impartiality seems to us proved, supposing that the facts are as he states them. But as he seems to be proud of having introduced the realism of Zola into English literature, we fail to see the justice of his complaint that he has met with exceptional treatment in his new venture. To be excluded from Mudie's, and to be bought instead of being borrowed, is the very distinction which he ought to have desired. His pamphlet has not changed our opinion concerning the character of his novel.' Yet, of the justice and utility of Moore's crusade no doubt could be entertained by anyone who could see beyond the frontiers of Mrs. Grundy's empire and had enough common sense to realize the artificiality of the three-volume system of publication. With the passing of years, Moore saw his role as historic and his pamphlet as a landmark in the evolution of the cultural climate of the 'eighties and 'nineties. He missed no opportunity of assailing the enemy even after the latter had surrendered – he did so in his preface to Zola's *Pot-Bouille (Piping Hot),* in his *Confessions of a Young Man* (1888) and again at the time of *Esther Waters* when W. H. Smith's, not Mudie's this time, refused to circulate a novel in which an unmarried Christian young lady was delivered of a child. By 1894 however, the scales had turned, and W. H. Smith's banning of the book proved to be a Pyrrhic victory which is said to have cost them some £1,500. After that, as Edwin Gilcher records in his biography of Moore, we can still see him clashing swords with the ghosts of Mudie's and Smith's in *Avowals* (1919) and in *A Communication to My Friends* (1933), a posthumous volume.

Time has not disproved the arguments of Moore in his war against the libraries, but his diagnosis of the malady of the novel and his remedy for it call for some qualifications. He is right in his analysis of the libraries' dictatorial rule, but he makes them responsible for sins of which publishers and many authors were also guilty. Exaggeration tempted him sorely. Who can agree with him that no English novel written between 1875 and 1885 would live through a generation? The names of Meredith, Hardy, George Eliot, Trollope and Stevenson come to mind as just a few to contradict his thesis, and the next decade offers some more names that won lasting recognition despite the continuation of the library-supported system. Moore is, however, right in his demonstration that Mudie, a tradesman wrapped up in his concern with public morality and ignorant of the demands of art, wielded inordinate power, as did the anonymous matrons and young persons in their provincial backwater. His extracts from contemporary novels published by the kings and queens of the circulating libraries demonstrate beyond the possibility of contradiction that his own novels offered no more 'offensive' matter than those of Mrs. Campbell-Praed, W. H. Mallock, Robert Buchanan or Ouida. He is right again when asserting that romantic and sentimental stories may well exercise a worse influence on young minds than novels that merely attempt to depict reality as it is. His arguments against the commercial and social-cultural consequences of three-volume publication are sound, yet he overlooks many of its nefarious consequences on the art of the novel – multiplicity of plots, protracted psychological analysis, vapid dialogue, and perhaps worst of all, the fostering of mediocre talent that could live on such a system because a printing of a few hundred copies made a book profit-earning for the publisher. The *Daily News* drew attention to this point in a leader on 3 July, 1871, declaring that England could be regarded 'as the Paradise of inefficient or unknown novelists'.

In his comments on Moore's article in the *Pall Mall Gazette* his contemporary, George Gissing, placed the question in a different perspective. Not that he fundamentally disapproved of Moore's campaign, though he disliked his style as he had disliked *A Modern Lover*. Yet he thought that novelists would be well advised to sweep the dirt off their own doorsteps. He himself fought down the prejudices of publishers and libraries against his own work, and though he never conquered the mass of the reading public, he did eventually defeat the reticences of publishing firms against his modern subjects, his realism and his pessimistic outlook on life. Following his own advice, he was true to his mission and together with Hardy, he largely contributed to the restoration of the dignity of the novel. His letter to the *Pall Mall Gazette* (reprinted here) suggests a remedy which could not appeal much to Moore. George Bernard Shaw, on his part, viewed the situation from yet another angle. He considered that it was the publishers (with the blessing of the libraries) who were responsible for the inordinate length of English novels. Inexpensive first editions in one volume were *the* solution, not guerilla warfare against Mudie's and Smith's. The publishers, he contended, must be persuaded to bring out novels in single-volume form. To the modern reader, the three writers' points of view appear to be equally pertinent, indeed quite complementary. Moore fought the libraries as citadels of repressive moralism, as commercial concerns dictating the format and the contents of novels to authors, publishers and reading public. The solution he advocated coincided with Shaw's suggestion in that both men thought that the libraries must be bypassed. Although admittedly less practical in appearance, Gissing's advocacy of greater artistic integrity on the novelists' part aimed at the same goal. After all, the libraries only circulated the books that writers were willing to write or capable of writing. Gissing saw the writer as the spring-head of literature – the source from which reform must proceed. If the better kind of novelists were determined to adopt a dignified and sincere course, they would gradually impose their views on publishers and circulating libraries alike.

Ultimately the conflict between novelists and libraries was resolved in a way which neither Moore nor Gissing nor Shaw had predicted. The spread of education resulting from Forster's 1870 Education Act affected the publishing world increasingly in the 1880s and 1890s. A demand for books was felt which could not be satisfied by the rigid, class-ridden system that Mudie had raised to the status of an institution. All publishers sought a larger market for the novels on their lists, printing one-volume editions ever sooner after the triple-decker issue. Experiments of single-volume first editions like those published by Vizetelly also multiplied in the late 'eighties and the 'nineties. The new firms in particular were keen on launching series which ignored the libraries' demand for triplets. Besides, an increasing number of authors came openly to repudiate the limitations imposed by the libraries – indeed some writers, like Kipling and Morley Roberts who started writing in the late 'eighties, never published in the orthodox format. Suddenly in 1894 the crisis came to a head.

The Society of Authors circulated among its members a pamphlet marked 'Private and Confidential' and entitled *The Three-Volume Novel,* which was an attack on the venerable three-decker. It reflected the growing dissatisfaction with an obsolete method of publishing which survived only 'by grace of Mudie'. The libraries in turn reacted: as they could hardly raise subscription rates, they warned publishers that they would henceforth pay no more than 4s. a volume for fiction, and they demanded that new cheaper editions should not be brought out until a year after the first. Such conditions could satisfy neither publishers nor authors. They obviously did not serve the interests of the reading public either. Mudie now admitted privately that he would be 'heartily glad and much relieved if the gods [i.e. the publishers] will give us the one volume from the first'. So, within a few years the three-volume novel tottered to its fall. According to Joseph Shaylor, the annual figure passed from 184 in 1894 to 52 in 1895, 25 in 1896 and only 4 in 1897. After that, the multi-volume issue was nothing more than a freak.

To declare, as A. Edward Newton did in *This Book-Collecting Game,* that 'it is to George Moore, rather than to any other man that we owe the one-volume novel, printed on good paper, in clear, legible type, and at a price within our reach', is an obvious overstatement Moore's struggle with the circulating libraries and their love for the tripartite form *was* significant; it *was* instrumental in the sinking of the three-decker. But his attacks only widened the hole in its side. The ship – *noblesse oblige* – was eventually scuttled by the captain.

Pierre Coustillas

PART TWO

The Debate in the Pall Mall Gazette

A New Censorship of Literature

In the many articles that have been lately written on the very vexed question of what is right and what is wrong in literature, one important point has on all sides been conceded: it is that of late years English fiction has sunk to an appallingly low ebb. Yet, although readily admitting that nothing beyond the value of a sentimental tale is to be found in the circulating libraries, apparently it has occurred to no one to seek for the reason of the alarming want of backbone in the novel of today. The writers who have devoted their attention to this question have preferred to offer advice and instruction as to how good work is to be produced. With the canons of art as laid down by Mr. Henry James and Mr. Besant I have no fault to find; I think them all excellent, but, while applauding the good counsel to 'go to nature and study it,' I cannot refrain from saying: 'Yes, yes; but we cannot do what you advise. The Oceanides might as well tell Prometheus to go away from the vulture that is tearing at his entrails. What is nature but religion and morals? and the circulating library forbids discussion on such subjects.' The subtraction of these two important elements of life throws the reading of fiction into the hands of young girls and widows of sedentary habits; for them political questions have no interest, and it is by this final amputation that humanity becomes headless, trunkless, limbless, and is converted into the pulseless, non-vertebrate, jelly-fish sort of thing which, securely packed in tin-cornered boxes, is sent from the London depot and scattered through the drawing-rooms of the United Kingdom. To make sure of a monopoly, this system, by using gradual pressure, forced the publishers to issue their books in three volumes, thereby getting rid of all purchasers, and securing to itself an absolute dictatorship in library matters. What it disapproves of comes into the world, as it were, stillborn; for no book is reissued in a cheap form that has not been in the first instance a success at the libraries. At the head, therefore, of English literature, sits a tradesman, who considers himself qualified to decide the most delicate artistic question that may be raised, and who crushes out of sight any artistic aspiration he may deem pernicious. And yet with this vulture gnawing at their hearts writers gravely discuss the means of producing good work; let them break their bonds first, and it will be time when they are free men to consider the possibilities of formulating a new aestheticism. Stories of the arbitrary decisions, of the intolerant spirit, of the worthy man whom we shall call Mr. X — every publisher's office is full of; but as I know none more striking, nor the truth of which I can so well vouch for, as my own, I will give it.

Last year I published a novel called *A Modern Lover.* The *Athenaeum* went out of its way to say that it was not immoral; the *Spectator* coincided in that view, and applauded through two columns. The other papers followed suit, and the book was spoken of in two articles, dealing with the present outlook in fiction, published in the *Fortnightly* and *Macmillan's.* On the strength of this I confess I expected on my return to London to meet a smiling publisher, and to be shown a satisfactory balance-sheet. But nothing of the sort; my reception was the reverse of what I had anticipated, and I was told that, commercially speaking, my book had been a failure. 'How, why, what do you mean?' I indignantly asked. 'You never published a book that was better reviewed, that was more liked.' 'Very possibly,' replied the publisher, 'but then Mr. X— set his foot on it: he had fifty copies and would not circulate them. He said it was immoral.' 'He couldn't have said so,' I cried. 'On what grounds? No newspaper said so.' 'I can't argue with you, I tell you the facts; and if you knew as much about publishing as I do, you'd believe them readily enough.' A cab soon took me up to Mr. X—'s place of business, and on presenting my card I was shown into the great man's private office. After a few words explaining who I was and the nature of my visit, I asked him why he had suppressed my book. 'I did not suppress your book,' he answered; 'I have some copies still in stock.' 'I dare say you have; but you only took fifty, whereas Mr. B— took three times that number, and I believe I am correct in stating that it is your custom to take twice as many as he.' Here commercial pride conquered prudence and Mr. X— said, 'I generally take three times as many as Mr. B—'. 'Well then, I should like to know why my case proved such an unfortunate exception to the rule?' 'Your book,' said Mr. X—, 'was considered immoral. Two ladies from the country wrote to me objecting to that scene where the girl sat to the artist as a model for Venus. After that I naturally refused to circulate your book, unless any customer said he wanted particularly to read Mr. Moore's novel.'

'But, my dear Sir, the *Spectator* selected and quoted the very scene you object to as the best in the book, as the most worthy of praise. You surely don't want to find fault with the morals of the *Spectator*.' Mr. X— hesitated, and sought for words. After a long silence he said, 'I saw the review in the *Spectator*, but I must consult the wishes of my clients.' 'Then am I to understand that the entire opinion of the press is to be set aside, and that it is the taste of two ladies in the country that controls the destinies of English literature?' 'I cannot undertake to discuss that question with you; all I can say is that we must consult the wishes of our customers.' 'I quite admit that such is your duty, but at the same time I cannot consent to have my work suppressed by the judgment of an unknown and irresponsible tribunal. I come to you now for a very definite purpose. 'A Modern Lover' is a spoilt book; don't let's talk any more about it, but concerning my next book, what are you going to do? Will you agree to be guided as regards my literary morals by the verdict of the *Spectator,* the *Athenaeum,* or would you prefer the *Academy*?' 'I can accept no opinion except that of my customers.' 'But I don't know who your customers are, and you only define them as two ladies in the country. I want something more definite; will you set up your own moral standard, and then I shall know up to what point I shall have to live?' 'I have no standard to set up; I shall take the advice of my customers.' 'Then Mr. X—, I shall publish my next book in a cheap form and challenge a popular verdict.' 'I am afraid,' he answered, 'you will find it difficult to persuade a publisher to issue your book in any other form than in three volumes.'

Comment on the above would be superfluous. He who runs may read, and none will fail to understand the mock-moral quagmire into which our literature is sinking – is being engulfed. Why our leading writers have not before now tried to extricate themselves from the intolerable jurisdiction of a tradesman I cannot say. Surely there are many among them who have something to say on the moral and religious feeling of their day? But with others I have nothing to do. My course at least is clear, for notwithstanding Mr. X—'s ghastly prophecy I have been fortunate enough to find a publisher willing to issue *A Mummer's Wife* at 6s.; 4s. 6d. at a discount bookseller's – still too high a price, in my opinion, but undoubtedly a great literary improvement on the thirty-one-and-sixpenny system. I shall now, therefore, for the future enjoy the liberty of speech granted to the journalist, the historian, and the biographer, rights unfortunately in the present day denied to the novelist. Whether others will follow my example, whether others will see as I see that the literary battle of our time lies not between the romantic and realistic schools of fiction, but for freedom from the illiterate censorship of a librarian, the next few years will most assuredly decide. I do not fear for the result. My only regret is that a higher name than mine has not undertaken to wave the flag of Liberalism and to denounce and to break with a commercial arrangement that makes of the English novel a kind of advanced school-book, a sort of guide to marriage and the drawing-room.

10 December, 1884, pp. 1–2

Correspondence

To the Editor *of the* Pall Mall Gazette

Sir – What do you think of the following, as illustrating the interesting article that appeared in the *Pall Mall Gazette* of yesterday?

> 'Max O'Rell writes in a spirit of friendliness and appreciation; there are many writers in England who, while flattering themselves that they have penetrated all kinds of feminine mysteries, are really far more ignorant of the subject than Max O'Rell, who, on this point, compares favourably

with by far the greater number of our English novelists.'

Standard

'In dealing with our womankind, Max O'Rell has shown sufficient gallantry to work more carefully, and consequently has produced a better book than before.'

Daily News

'It is with no small regret that we come to the end of this most diverting book, one of the very best works of its kind ever penned. It is temperate, logical, amusing ...'

Society

'Max O'Rell is not ill-natured or venomous; but he shows a complete inability to understand the English feminine character, or the true place of women in our social organism.' *Scotsman*

'The success of "John Bull et son Ile" has led Max O'Rell to publish a second volume, under the title of "Les Filles de John Bull," which, like most continuations is a failure.'

Athenaeum

> 'From beginning to end, there is not a particle of humour in the whole book.'
>
> *Saturday Review*

I will stop here, but I could fill your sixteen valuable pages with such [two] columns. I might translate Figaro's remarks, 'Loué par ceux-ci, blâmé par ceux-là, je me moque des sots, et fais la barbe à tout le monde,' by, 'Praised by the dailies, blamed by the weeklies, damned by British Podsnapery, but read by the public, I should feel very dull but for some highly amusing criticisms.'
I am, Sir, your obedient servant,

December 11 MAX O'RELL

(12 December, 1884, p.2)

To the Editor *of the* Pall Mall Gazette

Sir – Mr. Moore may be solaced when he hears that he is not alone in his 'top-shelf' exile. With him is Mr. Marion Crawford (!), for 'we prefer not to circulate "To Leeward" unless specially asked for.' The 'Catherine Daner' volume is also doled out very carefully with a word of kindly warning that it is 'very scandalous.' But, to crown all, on asking for a small primer by Professor Stuart, M.P., the ever vigilant assistant warned me that he was an atheist.

I am Sir, your obedient servant,

December 11 A READER

(12 December, 1884, p. 2)

To the Editor *of the* Pall Mall Gazette

Sir – The striking similarity of my own case to that of Mr. George Moore, pithily and powerfully told by him in your issue of 10th, induces me to send you this letter in the sincere hope that you may, by publishing it, help to remove a sore grievance. 'L'union fait la force;' and as it will require a great deal of 'force' to break the unwholesome 'ring' formed by 'Mr. X.,' of the circulating library, I add my testimony to that of the author of 'A Modern Lover,' in the hope that others similarly situated may do the same. My book 'Enslaved' was well reviewed by the *Athenaeum, Court Journal,* etc., and was briskly asked for at Mr. X.'s, who, however, instead of freely circulating the copies he had, sent half of them back to the publishers with a note informing them that he had received complaints from two customers as to the religious and moral complexion of the work. The other half, he agreed to circulate 'if specially asked for,' which, as I have had reason to learn, means something very like refusing the book to everybody. 'We have not a single copy on hand for the moment,' such is the invariable formula of the employé, 'but we can recommend this' – and here the young man offers the customer some admirable specimen of the 'jelly fish' novel, excellent reading (bar, very often, style and grammar) for the schoolroom, not to say the nursery. Shall I be considered too bold if I suggest that novels are not written exclusively for young ladies in their teens, that it is difficult to write a work of fiction such as mine, treating of Egypt and Turkey, while strictly conforming to the 'Country Curate and Lawn Tennis' style of thing, which Mr. X. hall-marks with the nod of approval and the smile of his piercing literary discernment? Everything which departs ever so little from the beaten track is sure to find opponents, and a novel is no exception to the rule. That the novel, however, should be virtually withdrawn from circulation because two persons out of perhaps two thousand who have read it condemn, is 'representing the minority' with a vengeance. There are those who love to stand forth as censors and to be able to say, 'I at once wrote to express my disapproval. I thought it due to myself and my position.' Such people are ever on the watch for a chance of posing as paragons; it flatters their vanity and lends them a certain reputation for uprightness in their little circle. Again, there are those well-meaning but imbecile people who would blush to mention the 'naked' eye, and who would fain adorn the legs of their pianos with drawers; but is the vast majority to suffer for such as these? The English public with its healthy tone may be relied upon to condemn a novel if it be unhealthy; but let them at least have the chance of judging for themselves. Again, if the dissenting voices of two are to damn a book, what an opening is there for the dagger-thrust of private malice and jealousy! The monopoly of the circulating library is both unjust and cruel; much more unwholesome than many of the books that its proprietor withers with his frown; for it cramps the field of fiction as a Chinese shoe cramps a Chinese lady's foot, making the unhappy wearer weak, tottering, and vapid.

I am, Sir, your obedient servant,

London, Dec. 13 ROBERT LANGSTAFF DE HAVILLAND

(13 December, 1884, p. 2)

To the Editor *of the* Pall Mall Gazette

Sir – Mr. George Moore's article on 'A new Censorship of Literature' is so evidently the utterance of a personal grievance that it can well be excused for being somewhat difficult of analysis as to composition, somewhat unreasonable or illogical in its arguments, and somewhat hasty in its charges. But those whom the circulating library system helps may state their case, as well as those who say that system harms them. Great as Mr. Moore's works undoubtedly are, and great as are innumerable others of the same calibre, I question if many of us would care to encumber our bookshelves with what of that kind a guinea a year would purchase after publication in the 'cheapest' form. The circulating library gives us the means of choosing as to what of modern fiction and of modern literature generally we will keep by us and set alongside the work of the masters. For, having read, we can in a short time turn to the list of surplus books at the library and find we may purchase at a reasonable price those that we care to keep; as, for example, I find by good luck to-day I can obtain for the modest sum of two shillings the original edition of Mr. Moore's 'A Modern Lover.' And the circulating library system enables us to do for ourselves what otherwise only the critic and those who have time to go to large public libraries – the British Museum reading-room and the like – could do; namely, read and refer to books which, either as to quality or quantity, would be far beyond the means of most of us to buy, and unsuitable for all but the owners of libraries that are exceptionally roomy to possess. It enables us alike to read all that is worth reading without forcing us to extravagance in loading our shelves, or to inconvenience by blocking up our chambers, and to escape, after boldly running the risk of reading what is worthless, the trouble of disposing of waste paper. Whoever 'X' the unknown in Mr. Moore's article may be, we may be sure he studies, and justifiably, the business portion of the work he undertakes; and the author who is reasonable will see that he himself, as far as the public is concerned, may or may not be a genius, but is unquestionably a trader; and unless, with a generosity scarcely known to fame, he presses his volumes upon the public bookshelves 'free, gratis, and for nothing,' and runs the risk of criticism alone, he must be content to run the risks natural to trade.

I am, Sir, your obedient servant,

December 12 J. W.

(13 December, 1884, p. 2)

To the Editor *of the* Pall Mall Gazette

Sir – I am not an old lady; and though I have a daughter, she is, happily, yet in her cradle. I am neither an author, a publisher, librarian, nor a parson. As a disinterested and dispassionate observer, then, I feel tempted to say a word or two about what Max O'Rell and Mr. Moore have said to us through your columns. When 'Les Filles de John Bull' appeared in Paris, the correspondent of the *Daily News* noticed it, remarking that it was more 'gaulois' than its forerunner. And he was not wrong. Now, there are some of us who can't translate 'l'esprit gaulois' into ear-pleasing English. Without being prudes, we object to pruriency. I have read many French novels, including some which come into the category not inaptly characterized as 'Studies in a Monkey House.' But 'Les Filles de John Bull' is more gravely offensive than them all. The Saturday reviewer meted to it its deserts when he criticised the book adversely and abstained from giving its title. Mr. Moore is very angry with some nameless one. And why, forsooth? Because Mr. Moore chooses to write books which ordinary English readers do not care to read. Why must we have thrust on us the mere dishwater from the banquets of MM. les Réalistes, of whom even their own compatriots, it is rumoured, are beginning to grow weary? Haven't we enterprising publishers ready to supply us with the real thing, under its own title, and illustrated to boot? Why should we have thrust on us books that neither profit nor divert, merely that a morbid-minded man may have the money on which to batten and nourish his unwholesome imaginings? Let him take a spade, rather, and go dig: 'Give earth yourself, go up for gain above!'

I am, Sir, your obedient servant,

December 13 SYLVANUS

(15 December, 1884 p. 2)

To the Editor *of the* Pall Mall Gazette

Sir – In affording Mr. Moore an opportunity of explaining in your columns the practical position of an English novelist who studies from life you have performed an essential service, not to a school alone, but to the cause of art, for the issues of the present discussion are far-reaching; but has not the author of 'A Mummer's Wife' lost a little by directing his indignation in the wrong quarter? The circulator of books is a tradesman, to be sure, and it is galling to have one's works hindered of their possible influence by his supervision; but what does the fact of such trading supervision imply, if not that the prevailing taste of the public has made it indispensable to success in the circulating business? Mr. Moore, of course, implies this in complaining that 'the destinies of literature' are controlled by mere considerations of profit and loss; would it not, however, be of more value to recognize that the course of literature is really directed by the men who make literature – that, in other words, of art decay among us, we must, in an age like ours, blame the artists? If you abolish the library system to-morrow, you are no nearer persuading the 'two ladies in the country' (typical beings!) to let this or that original work lie on their drawing-room tables; if you introduce forthwith the system of cheap first editions, you are no nearer improving the state of things, unless you can find literary men with power and courage to produce original books.

English novels are miserable stuff for a very miserable reason, simply because English novelists fear to do their best lest they should damage their popularity, and consequently their income. One of the most painful confessions in literature is that contained in the preface to 'Pendennis,' where Thackeray admits that 'since the author of "Tom Jones" was buried no writer of fiction among us has been permitted to depict to his utmost power a man,' on penalty, be it understood, of a temporary diminution of receipts. If this be not a tradesman's attitude, what is? Let novelists be true to their artistic conscience, and the public taste will come round. In that day there will be no complaint of the circulating libraries. It is a hard thing to say, but Thackeray, when he knowingly wrote below the demands of his art to conciliate Mrs. Grundy, betrayed his trust; and the same thing is being done by our living novelists every day.

I am, Sir, your obedient servant,

December 13 GEORGE GISSING

(15 December, 1884, p. 2)

To the Editor *of the* Pall Mall Gazette

Sir – I have a much heavier grievance against the librarian than either of your correspondents. I complain that his peculiar system spoils the sale of books most effectually, and that he applies that system of censorship not merely to the morals, but to the politics of authors. Take my own case. About six years ago I published, through one of the most respectable firms in London, a political biography in two volumes. It might have been sold at 24s., and at that price would have left a handsome profit, the actual cost of production being, as my publisher informed me, 15s. Had it been published at that price it would, I believe, have had a large sale, since, with the usual 'twopence in the shilling discount,' the price would have been an even sovereign. Solely because of the pressure put upon the publishers by the libraries, the price was raised to 32s., with, as I need hardly say, disastrous results to the sale. There is, however, worse to come. The book had scarcely been out three months when it figured in the front page of the catalogues of surplus books at a little more than half-price, and the sale, which though slow had been steady, at once fell off to almost nothing. The pecuniary loss to myself – I taking the greater part of the price in royalties – was very considerable; and I suffered further by the delay in bringing out a second edition, for which my publishers had requested me to prepare. I may add that more than one of my friends, on asking for the book, were warned of its political tendencies.

I am, Sir, your obedient servant,

December 13

AUCTOR

(16 December, 1884, p. 2)

To the Editor *of the* Pall Mall Gazette

Sir – Mr. Moore and your correspondents seem to be misleading themselves and each other. All they have written only proves that there is but one market for the thirty-one shilling and sixpenny three-volume novel, a fact not surprising considering that such works are generally scampered through in an afternoon, and certainly have no recommendation for the library shelf. Mr. N is not a censor. He simply says: I am the only person who can trade in the cumbersome, expensive things you are so foolish as to produce. Therefore I shall buy or reject where I please. Authors are in no difficulty on this account. Hundreds of thousands of copies of 'Called Back' have been sold, and we are informed by Saturday's papers that 160,000 of 'Dark Days' have already been distributed. At the nominal price of one shilling each these will probably pay both publisher and writer far better than the unnecessarily bulky and inconvenient three volumes. Authors need but supply at an unprohibitive price what the public wants, and they will be able to dispense altogether with the offices of the go-between or book circulating agent.

I am, Sir, your obedient servant,

December 13 JAMES DAVIS

(16 December, 1884, p. 2)

The Case for the Publishers

The correspondence excited by Mr. George Moore's letter on the New Censorship of Literature continues unabated. From a number of letters received this morning we select the following, sent us by a member of one of the leading publishing firms in London, as representing that side of the question which has been least heard at present:–

The 'wrongs of authors' make their appearance in the newspapers with a wonderful regularity. Their form varies from time to time, but their substance is ever the same. In your issue of Thursday last they are formulated under three heads – (1) that authors are not paid enough for their work; (2) that they have no means of knowing whether they get even their stipulated share of profits. (3) That they are kept a long time waiting for their money. To No. 1 I would reply that a great many authors are utterly unreasonable in their expectations; they appear to be possessed by a conviction that because their work is printed and issued for sale it must prove a financial success, or at least pay the expenses of production. If they learn that it has not done so, they immediately blame their publishers. I think most publishers will agree with me in stating that the authors who as a rule give the most trouble, and have the largest expectations, are those who produce the least valuable works. A weekly journal has recently published a rather bitter attack on circulating libraries, and has thrown the entire blame of the 'three-volume novel' on them. I am not disposed to take up the cudgels on behalf of either the circulating libraries or three-volume novels, but I consider that the inordinate expectations of the authors of trivial works of fiction have, in conjunction with a certain want of discrimination among publishers – to which I propose to allude further on – constituted one of the chief factors in the evolution of that essentially modern English production the three-volume novel.

As to wrong No. 2, authors are given to very hasty generalization. In the publishing trade, as in other trades and professions, there are no doubt, harpies; but if an author has fallen into the hands of one of them it is rather hard that the whole class should be included in a sweeping condemnation. If a certain doctor has failed to cure that author, or if he has been robbed by his solicitor, he does not condemn the whole of the learned professions. There are publishers who are ready to give every reasonable assurance to a suspicious author that he is being fairly dealt with, but the general experience of such publishers is that their personal character is in 99 cases out of 100 considered a sufficient guarantee – as is usual in dealings between gentlemen.

With regard to wrong No. 3 your correspondent admits that all publishers do not take the same morals of grace. Is he aware that some publishers pay their authors in cash on making up the annual accounts? If the publisher is paid quarterly by the bookseller, or monthly as your correspondent states, he has to give discount for the money so received, while the author is paid in full – in some cases even before the money so paid him has been received by the publisher.

One charge, I admit, may be brought against publishers as a class, and that is a want of discrimination in the works they undertake. If nothing were accepted which did not present some prospect, or even a bare possibility, of success, there would be less disappointment, and less ill-feeling on the part of the authors. Publishers should, in fact, make it their aim to pay authors and not to be paid by them. But if publishers lack discrimination in what they undertake, still more, I venture to think, do many of the critics of today lack discrimination in the selection of books to be noticed and books to be praised. As your own paper is one of the notable exceptions to this rule, I have the less hesitation in alluding to the subject. Every publisher knows that the MSS submitted to him group themselves under three heads – (1) a small minority, the absolutely good, which he unhesitatingly accepts; (2) a somewhat larger minority, the absolutely worthless – worthless beyond a possibility of doubt – which he as unhesitatingly rejects, and (3) the large majority which comprises what Professor Tyndall would call the 'penumbral zone' between the good and the worthless; of this class some are accepted and some are referred elsewhere. Now, even the absolutely worthless seldom fail to see the light somewhere. And I venture to think that the critics might exercise a much greater restraint on the publication of 'trash' than they do. I am fully alive to the many obstacles to perfect independence in such matters which exist, but I think that many of them might be removed or ignored, and that a great service would thus be rendered to literature. Another grievance that the author and publisher alike may plead is the amount of piracy which is committed at the present time. If a man has with great research and trouble written a biography (possibly after having first 'discovered' his hero), or a history, or a text book which has made its mark, an epitome of the life or a 'popular history' or a 'concise manual' is pretty sure to make its appearance, so carefully adapted as to evade the law of copyright, but seriously to injure the original work. It is obviously inexpedient for me to cite examples, but I have little doubt that your readers will be able to supply them for themselves. I would submit these grievances to the consideration of the Society of Authors.

(17 December, 1884, pp. 1–2)

PART THREE

Literature at Nurse, or Circulating Morals

by George Moore

PRICE THREEPENCE

Literature at Nurse

OR

CIRCULATING MORALS

BY GEORGE MOORE

AUTHOR OF "A MUMMER'S WIFE," "A MODERN LOVER," ETC.

"They stand there, Respectable; and—what more? Dumb idols; with a skin of delusively-painted waxwork, inwardly empty, or full of rags and bran. . . . Such bounties, in this as in infinitely deeper matters, does Respectability shower down on us. Sad are thy doings, O Gig; sadder than those of Juggernaut's Car: that, with huge wheel, suddenly crushes asunder the bodies of men; thou in thy light-bobbing Long-acre springs, gradually winnowest away their souls!"

. . . .

"One day the *Mudie* mountain, which seemed to stand strong like the other rock mountains, gave suddenly, as the icebergs do, a loud-sounding crack; suddenly, with huge clangour, shivered itself into ice dust; and sank, carrying much along with it."—*Carlyle's Essays.*

LONDON

VIZETELLY & CO., 42 CATHERINE STREET, STRAND

1885

LITERATURE AT NURSE,

OR

CIRCULATING MORALS.

THIS paper should have been offered to *The Nineteenth Century*, but as, for purely commercial reasons, it would be impossible for any English magazine to print it, I give it to the public in pamphlet form.

In an article contributed to the *Pall Mall Gazette* last December, I called attention to the fact that English writers were subject to the censorship of a tradesman who, although doubtless an excellent citizen and a worthy father, was scarcely competent to decide the delicate and difficult artistic questions that authors in their struggles for new ideals might raise: questions that could and should be judged by time alone. I then proceeded to show how, to retain their power, the proprietors of the large circulating libraries exact that books shall be issued at extravagant prices, and be supplied to them at half the published rate, or even less, thus putting it out of the power of the general public to become purchasers, and effectually frustrating the right of the latter to choose for themselves.

The case, so far as I am individually concerned, stands thus: In 1883, I published a novel called "A Modern Lover." It met with the approval of the entire press; *The Athenæum* and *The Spectator* declared emphatically that it was not immoral; but Mr. Mudie told me that two ladies in the country had written to him to say that they disapproved of the book, and on that account he could not circulate it. I answered, "You are acting in defiance of the opinion of the press—you are taking a high position indeed, and one from which you will probably be overthrown. I, at least, will have done with you; for I shall find a publisher willing to issue my next book at a purchasable price, and so enable me to appeal direct to the public." Mr. Mudie tried to wheedle, attempted to dissuade me from my rash resolution; he advised me to try another novel in three volumes. Fortunately I disregarded his suggestion, and my next book, "A Mummer's Wife," was published at the price of six shillings. The result exceeded my expectations, for the book is now in its fourth edition. The press saw no immoral tendency in it, indeed *The Athenæum* said that it was "remarkably free from the elements of uncleanness." Therefore it is not with a failing but with a firm heart that I return to the fight—a fight which it is my incurable belief must be won if we are again to possess a literature worthy of the name. This view of the question may be regarded by some as quixotic, but I cannot forget that my first article on the subject awakened a polemic that lasted several weeks, giving rise to scores of articles and some hundreds of paragraphs. The *Saturday Review* wrote, "Michel Lévy saved France with cheap publications, who will save England?" Thus encouraged, I yield again to the temptation to speak upon a subject which on such high authority is admitted to be one of national importance. Nor do I write influenced by fear of loss or greed of gain. The "select" circulating libraries can no longer injure me; I am now free to write as I please, and whether they take or refuse my next novel is to me a matter of indifference. But there are others who are not in this position, who are still debutants, and whose artistic aspirations are being crushed beneath the wheels of these implacable Juggernauts. My interest in the question is centred herein, and I should have confined myself to merely denouncing the irresponsible censorship exercised over literature if I did not hear almost daily that when "A Mummer's Wife" is asked for at Mudie's, and the assistants are pressed to say why the book cannot be obtained, they describe it as an immoral publication which the library would not be justified in circulating.

Being thus grossly attacked, it has occurred to me to examine the clothing of some of the dolls passed by our virtuous librarian as being decently attired, and to see for myself if there be not an exciting bit of bosom exhibited here and a naughty view of an ankle shown there; to assure myself, in fact, if all the frocks are modestly set as straight as the title Select Library would lead us to expect.

Perhaps of all moral theories, to do unto others as you would be done unto meets with the most unhesitating approval. Therefore my *confrères*, of whose works I am going to speak, will have nothing to complain of. I shall commence by indicating the main outlines of my story of "A Mummer's Wife," appending the passage that gained it refusal at Mudie's; then I shall tell the stories of three fashionable novels (all of which were, and no doubt still are, in circulation at Mudie's Select Library), appending extracts that will fairly set before the reader the kind of treatment adopted in each case. The public will thus be able to judge between Mr. Mudie and me.

Now as to "A Mummer's Wife." Kate Ede is the wife of an asthmatic draper in Hanley. Attending her husband's sick-bed and selling reels of cotton over the little counter, her monotonous life flows unrelieved by hope, love, or despair. To make a few extra shillings a week the Edes let their front rooms, which are taken by Mr. Dick Lennox, the manager of an opera bouffe company on tour. He makes love to the draper's wife, seduces her, and she elopes with him. She travels about with the actors, and gradually becomes one of them; she walks among the chorus, speaks a few words, says a few verses, and is eventually developed into a heroine of comic opera. The life, therefore, that up to seven-and-twenty knew no excitement, no change of thought or place, now knows neither rest nor peace. Even marriage—for Dick Lennox marries her when Ralph Ede obtains his divorce—is unable to calm the alienation of the brain that so radical a change of life has produced, and after the birth of her baby she takes to drink, sinks lower and lower until death from dropsy and liver complaint in a cheap lodging saves her from becoming one of the street-walkers with whom she is in the habit of associating. That is my story; here is the passage objected to:—

At last she felt him moving like one about to awake, and a moment after she heard him say, "There's Mr. Lennox at the door; he can't get in; he's kicking up an awful row. Do go down and open for him."

"Why don't you go yourself," she answered, starting into a sitting position.

"How am I to go? you don't want me to catch my death at that door?" Ralph replied angrily.

Kate did not answer, but quickly tying a petticoat about her, and wrapping herself in her dressing-gown, she went downstairs. It was quite dark and she had to feel her way along. At last, however, she found and pulled back the latch, but when the white gleam of moonlight entered she retreated timidly behind the door.

"I am sorry," said Dick, trying to see who was the concealed figure, "but I forgot my latch-key."

"It does not matter," said Kate.

"Oh, it is you, dear! I have been trying to get home all day, but couldn't. Why didn't you come down to the theatre?"

"You know that I can't do as I like."

"Well, never mind; don't be cross; give me a kiss."

Kate shrunk back, but Dick took her in his arms. "You were in bed then?" he said, chuckling.

"Yes, but you must let me go."

"I should like never to let you go again."

"But you are leaving to-morrow."

"Not unless you wish me to, dear."

Kate did not stop to consider the impossibility of his fulfilling his promise, and, her heart beating, she went upstairs. On the first landing he stopped her, and laying his hand on her arm, said, "And would you be really be very glad if I were to stay with you?"

"Oh, you know I would, Dick!"

They could not see each other. After a long silence she said, "We must not stop talking here. Mrs. Ede sleeps, you know, in the room at the back of the work-room, and she might hear us."

"Then come into the sitting-room," said Dick, taking her hands and drawing her towards him.

"Oh, I cannot!"

"I love you better than anyone in the world."

"No, no; why should you love me?"

Although she could not see his face she felt his breath on her neck. Strong arms were wound about her, she was carried forward, and the door was shut behind her.

Only the faintest gleam of starlight touched the wall next to the window: the darkness slept profoundly on the landing and staircase; and when the silence was again broken, a voice was heard saying, "Oh, you shouldn't have done this! What shall I tell my husband if he asks me where I've been?"

"Say you have been talking to me about my bill, dear. I'll see you in the morning."

The story of "Nadine," by Mrs. Campbell Praed, runs as follows:—Nadine, a young girl of twenty, is staying in a fashionable country house. There she meets Dr. Bramwell and Colonel Halkett, a married man; the latter she admits into her bedroom in the dead of night; he dies there of heart disease, and, in her nightdress, she is seen dragging the corpse down the passage by Dr. Bramwell. Next morning the servant informs the house that he has found Colonel Halkett dead in his bed. Dr. Bramwell examines the body, says nothing of what he has seen overnight, and there the matter for the present ends. But Dr. Bramwell is hopelessly in love with Nadine, and he meets her a few weeks after at a great ball in London. She begs of him to take her out into the garden. There they talk of Colonel Halkett's death, and Dr. Bramwell begs of Nadine to say that she tried to repulse the colonel; she declines to do so.

Six months after they meet again in the same country house where Colonel Halkett died. Dr. Bramwell is brooding over his love in the dead of night, when he is startled by a knock at the door. It is Nadine. At a glance he sees that she is in labour; she begs of him to come to her room and deliver her of the child. Next morning a nurse is called in. Dr. Bramwell, for the sake of Nadine, tells a tissue of falsehoods; he declares that she is suffering from a severe shock to her nervous system, and that her safety depends on nobody being admitted to her room. As soon as she possibly can Nadine gets away, leaving the child with Dr. Bramwell, who adopts it.

Years pass. Nadine meets a Russian prince at Nice, marries him, and comes to live in England. Dr. Bramwell falls in love with Miss Blundell, a friend of Nadine's, whose mother will not accept him as a suitor for her daughter's hand on account of the mystery that hangs about the parentage of his ward—Nadine's child. Dr. Bramwell goes to Nadine, begs of her to use her influence with Mrs. Blundell (Mrs. Blundell owes Nadine money) to make her consent to his marriage with her daughter. But instead Nadine talks to Dr. Bramwell of their past, and ends by proposing to become his mistress. After some hesitation he declines: Nadine turns upon him fiercely, and refuses to assist him in his endeavours to marry Miss Blundell; she denies ever having borne a child, and challenges him to do his worst. Dr. Bramwell returns home dumbfounded; but that night Nadine comes to his house repentant, holding a written confession in her hand. This is sent to Mrs. Blundell. The doctor marries the girl, and Nadine goes off to Russia with her husband.

The first extract I give is from the chapter entitled "In the Pavilion." Bramwell has led Nadine away from the dancers; he shows her a ring in proof of what he saw in the house at Croxham. Nadine faints. He tries to reanimate the motionless form:—

"Oh, Nadine," he murmured, "my love, my darling! you bade me be kind, and idiot-like, I have smitten you as though you were my enemy." He pressed his lips to hers in a transport of passion. Never before had he so forgotten himself. She opened her eyes, and he saw in them something of the same blank horror as had transfixed her features during that momentary flash of moonlight in the corridor at Croxham.

Then when Nadine recovers consciousness,

"There is one solution," he said hoarsely. "I have repeated it to myself so often, that it has become borne in upon me as truth, and has comforted me in my despair. Nadine, let me speak as though I were your brother. Trust in my loyalty, my reverence. That night—listen—is not this how it was? He forced his way into your room. You repulsed him. In the excitement and agitation death struck him."

Bramwell paused and waited breathlessly for her reply. None came. She sat motionless, her eyes bent downwards. In his agony he quitted her side and walked towards the door of the tent. Here he stood for several moments looking earnestly upon her, while there was still silence. At length the strain became unbearable, and he turned his face resolutely away from her. Aware of the movement, she seemed to interpret it as a sign of desertion. For a second the old defiance revived. She uplifted her head, her lips framed the words, "Go! think the worst of me that you choose; I can live without you."

Then when Nadine comes to Bramwell's room to ask him to deliver her of her child:—

Bramwell gave her admission; and she stood in his presence white and almost as terror-stricken as upon the night to which his thoughts now involuntarily reverted. She was dressed in a loose cashmere robe that, clinging to her form, displayed its outlines clearly. In an instant his practised intelligence had grasped her imminent need. His worst horror confronted him. She had come to him for aid in the direst extremity which can befall a woman. He stood, almost as pale as she was, waiting for her to speak. Suddenly she divined that he knew her secret. A wave of crimson swept over her face. She advanced with drooped eyes, and said in an imperative whisper, "I want you to come at once to my room." He bowed his head, and still without speaking followed her down the long dim corridor till they turned into the west wing. Here she paused, and motioned him to enter a room, the door of which stood partially open; then closed it behind them both and turned the key.

It being well known that I am no judge of such things, tell me, Mr. Mudie, if there be not in this doll just a little too much bosom showing, if there be not too much ankle appearing from under this skirt? Tell me, I beseech you.

The story of "A Romance of the Nineteenth Century," by W. H. Mallock, runs as follows:—

Ralph Vernon, a young man half philosopher, half poet, is living at Nice. There he meets Miss Walters, who had been seduced a year or two before by Colonel Stapleton.

The colonel has been away in Palestine, but he has returned to Europe, and when the story opens he also is staying at Nice. The grossness of the lines on which their sensual intercourse has been conducted is easily imagined when we are told that the colonel has generally in his pocket a collection of obscene photographs, which he shows to his acquaintances, and which he sends to Miss Walters, who in turn shows them to the religious sensualist, Mr. Vernon. The latter falls hopelessly in love with Miss Walters. He wastes his time in talking religion, and she reflects, "Were you all a man ought to be you would be able to love in a more human way than you do." Vernon, however, is unable to do this, and Miss Walters goes to see the colonel in a very pretty room which he has taken for the purpose in the Hotel Victoria. Meanwhile Vernon strives to console himself with a depraved married woman called Mrs. Crane. But the memory of Miss Walters haunts him, and, after indulging in much kissing, he resists temptation. Then, in the last chapter, all meet at a masquerade ball. Miss Walters takes Vernon away into the garden; she tells him that the colonel "has recovered all," and dies of heart disease in his arms. He, not knowing that she is dead, runs to dip his handkerchief in a fountain, but at that moment the colonel, singing a comic song, passes down the pathway, and Vernon (who is in the costume of a Spanish pedlar) seizes him by the throat; the colonel, fancying he is attacked by some vagrant, pulls out a revolver and shoots his assailant dead.

Here are a few extracts from one of the different love scenes between Vernon and Miss Walters:—

The temptation was too much for Vernon. He put his hand on her shoulder, and let it slip down to her waist. She made no struggle; he felt her yield to his touch; and, still holding her, he led her back to her seat.

"You are looking beautiful to-day," he murmured.

"I'm glad of that," she said. "I should like your last impressions to be nice of me. Don't you admire my rose too?"

It was in her button-hole, and Vernon stooped forward to smell it. As he was slowly drawing back, her breath stirred his hair. He raised his eyes, and his lips were close to hers. Neither of them spoke: they each drew a breath sharply: in another instant the outer world was dark to them, and their whole universe was nothing but a single kiss. . . . . Her lips parted a little, a flush stole over her cheek, she opened her arms as if to call him to herself, and at last, in a breathless whisper, she said "Come!" She saw that he did not stir, and she moved her head imperiously. "Come!" she repeated, "come closer. I want you here. There is something I wish to tell you."

He did as she commanded; he moved quite close to her, and in another instant her fair arms were round him, pressing him to her breathing bosom. Her lips were close to his ear. "My own one," she said, "I love you;" and still holding him, and almost in the same breath, "you must pay me," she said, "for having told you that. Kiss me—kiss me on the mouth, and say that you love me too." . . . At last her arms released him, and the two exchanged glances. "Tell me," she murmured, "are you happy now?"

"Yes, and no," he said; and there was then a long silence. "Cynthia, even yet you have not answered my question."

"What question?" she said. "Do you mean if I love goodness? Oh, if I do not yet (and she pressed his hand to her lips), you shall teach me to. You shall teach me everything. You shall do exactly what you will with me."

Notwithstanding, Vernon's love could not be sufficiently humanized, and at the end of the scene Colonel Stapleton is announced. This is how his arrival is led up to:—

"My memory is still full of the past; no magic can alter that; and if you went from me, and made a vacuum in my present, the past would probably rush in and fill it up."

"Listen to me," said Vernon, with a sudden coldness in his voice. "Let us suppose I am very fond of the smell of eau-de cologne. Do you think that if I had none left in my bottle, I should dip my pocket-handkerchief in the next drain as a substitute?"

"I think you would be very silly if you did," she said, her voice growing cold also.

"Then would you not be equally or even more silly, if, on losing a comrade in the search of the thing you loved, you were to try to console yourself by seeking the thing you hated?"

"Only, the worst of it is, you see," she said with a slight laugh, "that the things that would console me are not things I hate. If it were so, I should not be what I am. When drunkards have not got wine they will drink stuff out of the next spirit lamp." . . .

"What then is it? you are a complete mystery to me. If I only knew the truth, I could be of so much more help to you."

"Don't ask me," she said; "why harp upon this one subject? Is there any use in trying to stir up all the dregs of my nature? In all conscience I have told you enough already. Do you know," she went on with a smile of expiring tenderness, "you must be, I think, a very innocent-minded person, or you would have understood it pretty well by this time."

Soon after the servant announces that the colonel is in the drawing-room:—

"Tell him," she said, "that I am coming up immediately. I will be with him in a few minutes." She waited till the man (the servant) was out of sight, and then she rose to go. "Good morning, Mr. Vernon," she said coldly as she swept past him [her still unhumanized lover]. "I suppose I shall hardly see you again to-day—or, indeed, for some time to come—as we may possibly go to-morrow."

Then Vernon returns home in a state verging on stupor. He, however, writes to her, and begs of her to meet him again at the same place. She consents, and this time, it must be admitted, lost not a moment, and made every possible effort to humanize him to her satisfaction. He was about to speak, but she did not give him time:—

"Come," she said, "am I not looking well to-night? Why don't you kiss me and tell me how soft and pretty I am? Isn't that what you say generally when you talk to girls like me? By the way, I have found a word that will at least describe what I might have been, had circumstances only favoured me, an *hetaira*.* If I had lived in Athens I should have performed that part capitally. I was made for a life of pleasure, I think, if—, if—." She stopped abruptly for a moment, and then broke out once more, "If only there were not something in me that had made all my pleasure a hell."

But notwithstanding all this encouragement, Vernon lapses into religious talk—sermonings of all kinds—and in despair

* In English, *a prostitute*.

at not being able to make him understand her, she takes him up to the house, and shows him the obscene photographs. He is terribly shocked, and confesses his folly in "wishing her to become an innocent girl again."

"Amongst the highest saints in heaven," he says, "there will be faces deeply scarred by the battle. You are right, very likely, that there is no way back to Eden; but—I am not a great quoter of texts, yet I still remember this one—"We all die in Adam, but we may all live in Christ.'"

She asks him if he really believes what he says, and being assured that he does, in front of the obscene photographs that have fallen on the floor she kneels down and murmurs "Our Father;" he, staring at the stars and palm-trees, "wondered if prayer meant anything?"

After this scene the lovers are separated for some time, but Miss Walters sends her picture to Vernon; on looking at it he declares: "If she will not be God's she must and shall be mine!" She, while contemplating herself in the glass, said to herself, with her heart full of Vernon, "My body at least is worthy of your acceptance." But at that moment the servant brought her a telegram from the colonel, announcing his arrival by the next train:—

"Come," said he, "what on earth is the matter with you? You shouldn't treat me in this way, for I can only stay ten minutes. I have come over with some lawyer's papers for Molly Crane to sign, and in another half-hour I shall have to start for Nice again. I heard you were in the garden, so I couldn't help having one try at finding you."

The news that the Colonel was going gave Miss Walters great relief, and brought a smile to her face that was perhaps more cordial than she meant it to be, for the Colonel took her by the chin and turned her face towards him. At his touch, however, she started back abruptly, though the smile did not desert her.

"Remember, Jack," she said, "I'm going to have no more of your nonsense. We are too old, both of us, for that kind of thing."

"I'm not," said the Colonel, "though I believe at this moment, I'm in too great a hurry for it. However, I shall be back here to have another look at our Molly in a couple of days. I've engaged a room, a first-rate one, at the Hotel Victoria Such a view from it,

I can tell you! You must come," he went on, fixing his gleaming eyes on her, "and see it yourself one of these days, little cross vindictive minx that you are!"

It being well known that I am no judge of such things, tell me, Mr. Mudie, if there be not in this doll just a little too much bosom showing, if there be not just a little too much ankle appearing from under this skirt? Tell me, I beseech you.

The story of "Foxglove Manor," by Robert Buchanan, reeks of the pulpit and the alcove. The hero is a young parson who uses religion for the purpose of seducing his congregation—he, in fact, uses it very much in the same way as Colonel Stapleton did the obscene photographs. When he has ruined Miss Edith Dove he deserts her for Mrs. Haldane, who, after much kissing and tying of pocket-handkerchiefs round swollen ankles, is saved from him by the machinations of her husband, a great scientist. On leaving Mrs. Haldane, the Rev. Mr. Santley muses to the following effect:—

"I love this woman. In her heart she loves me. Her superior spiritual endowments are mystically alive to those I myself possess. Her husband is a clod, an unbeliever, with no spiritual promptings. In his sardonic presence, her aspirations are chilled, frozen at the fountain-head, whereas in mine, all the sweetness and the power of her nature are aroused, though with a certain irritation. If I persist, she must yield to the slow moral mesmerism of my passion, and eventually fall. Is this necessarily evil? Am I of set purpose sinning? Is it not possible that even a breach of the moral law might under certain conditions lead us both to a higher religious place—yes, even to a deeper and intenser consciousness of God?"

And again—

"What is sin? Surely it is better than moral stagnation, which is death. There are certain deflections from duty which, like the side stroke of a bird's wing, may waft us higher. In the arms of this woman I should surely be nearer God than crawling alone on the bare path of duty, loving nothing, hoping nothing, becoming nothing. What is it that Goethe says of the Eternal Feminine which leads us ever upwards and onwards? Which was the highest, Faust before he loved Marguerite, or Faust after he passed out of the shadow of his sin into the sphere of empirial and daring passion? I believe in God, I love this woman. Out of that belief, and that love, shall I not become a living soul?"

Later on in the book we find a meeting between our libidinous clergyman and his victim Miss Edith Dove, described as follows—

"She wore a light dress of some soft material, a straw hat, a country cloak, and gloves of Paris kid—a civilized nymph, as you perceive! To complete her modern appearance she carried a closed parasol and a roll which looked like music . . . And the satyr? Ah! I knew him at a glance, despite the elegant modern boots used to disguise the cloven foot. He wore black broadcloth and snowy linen, too, and a broad-brimmed clerical hat. His face was seraphically pale, but I saw (or fancied I saw), the twinkle of the hairy ears of the ignoble, sensual, nymph-compelling, naiad-pursuing breed."

In the third volume, in a chapter entitled "And lo! within her something leapt," the result of the love encounter is made known to the reader.

She arose shivering; and at that very instant there came to her a warning, an omen full of nameless terror. It seemed to her as if faces were flashing before her eyes, voices shrieking in her ears; her heart leapt, her head went round, and at the same moment she felt her whole being miraculously thrilled by the quickening of a new life within her own. With a loud moan, she fainted away upon the floor. When she returned to consciousness, she was lying nearly naked by the bedside and the moonlight was flooding the little room.

Now a writer like myself, whom you had proved to be no better than he should be, might be said to be capable of comparing a clergyman of the Church of England to a satyr, of even calling him "the snake of the parish," but you, Mr. Mudie, Methodist or Baptist, I forget which you are, how can you allow such a book in your Select Library? Two old ladies in the country wrote to you about my "Modern Lover," and you suppressed it; but did not one of the thousands of young ladies in the many thousand parsonages you supply with light literature write to tell you that papa was not "the snake of the parish," and your great friend the British Matron, did she never drop you a line on the subject? Tell me, I beseech you.

I say your great friend, my dear Mr. Mudie, because I wish to distinguish between you, for latterly your identities have got so curiously interwoven that it would need a critical insight that few—I may say none—possess, to separate you. Indeed on this subject many different opinions are afloat. Some hold that being the custodian of the national virtue you have by right adopted the now well-known signature as your *nom de plume,* others insist that the lady in question is your better half (by that is it meant the better half of your nature or the worthy lady who bears your name?), others insist that you yourself are the veritable British Matron. How so strange a belief could have obtained credence I cannot think, nor will I undertake to say if it be your personal appearance, or the constant communication you seem to be in with this mysterious female, or the singularly obtrusive way you both have of forcing your moral and religious beliefs upon the public that has led to this vexatious confusion of sex. It is, however, certain that you are popularly believed to be an old woman; and assuming you to be the British Matron I would suggest, should this pamphlet cause you any annoyance, that you write to *The Times* proving that the books I have quoted from are harmless, and differ nowise from your ordinary circulating corals whereon young ladies are supposed to cut their flirtation teeth. The British Matron has the public by the ear, and her evidence on the subject of impure literature will be as greedily listened to as were her views on painting from the nude. But although I am willing to laugh at you, Mr. Mudie, to speak candidly, I hate you; and I love and am proud of my hate of you. It is the best thing about me. I hate you because you dare question the sacred right of the artist to obey the impulses of his temperament; I hate you because you are the great purveyor of the worthless, the false and the commonplace; I hate you because you are a fetter about the ankles of those who would press forward towards the light of truth; I hate you because you feel not the spirit of scientific inquiry that is bearing our age along; I hate you because you pander to the intellectual sloth of to-day; I hate you because you would mould all ideas to fit the narrow limits in which your own turn; I hate you because you impede the free development of our literature. And now that I have told you what I think of you, I will resume my examination of the ware you have in stock.

Without in the least degree attempting to make an exhaustive list of the books which to my surprise this most virtuous literary tradesman consents to circulate, I may venture to call attention to "Puck," by Ouida. This is the history of a courtezan through whose arms, in the course of the narrative, innumerable lovers pass. "Moths," by the same author, tells how a dissolute adventuress sells to her lover the pure white body and soul of her daughter, and how in the end Vera, disgraced and degraded by her ignoble husband, goes off to live with the tenor with whom she fell in love at the beginning of the story. In a book I opened the other day at haphazard, "Phillida," by Florence Marryat, I find a young lady proposing to a young parson to be his mistress. It is true that the feelings that prompt her are not analysed, but does the cause of morals gain I wonder by this slightness of treatment?

It is not for me to put forward any opinion of my own. I have spoken of and quoted only from the works of writers longer and better known to the public than I am. They do not need defence against the Philistine charge of immorality, and it would be ridiculous for me—ostracised as I am by the founder and president of our English Academy, the Select Circulating Library—to accuse them, or even to hint that they have offended against the Mudie code more deeply than myself. I therefore say nothing. I cast no stone. All I seek is to prove how absurd and how futile is the censorship which a mere tradesman assumes to exercise over the literature of the nineteenth century, and how he overrules the decisions of the entire English press.

Were I indeed the only writer who has suffered from this odious tyranny the subject might well be permitted to drop. Many cases might be brought forward, but I will not look further than last month. I am informed on good authority that on being written to repeatedly for a book called "Leicester," Mr Mudie sent back word to the Athenæum Club that he did not keep naturalistic literature—that he did not consider it "proper." And thus an interesting, if not a very successful, literary experiment is stamped out of sight, and the strange paradox of a tradesman dictating to the bishops of England what is proper and improper for them to read is insolently thrust upon us. However the matter has been brought before the committee of the club, and the advisability of withdrawing the subscription from this too virtuous library is under consideration.

It has been and will be again advanced that it is impossible to force a man to buy goods if he does not choose to do so: but with every privilege comes a duty. Mr. Mudie possesses a monopoly, and he cannot be allowed to use that monopoly to the detriment of all interests but his own. But even if this were not so, it is no less my right to point out to the public, that the character for strength, virility, and purpose, which our literature has always held, the old literary tradition coming down to us through a long line of glorious ancestors, is being gradually obliterated to suit the commercial views of a narrow-minded tradesman. Instead of being allowed to fight, with and amid, the thoughts and aspirations of men, literature is now rocked to an ignoble rest in the motherly arms of the librarian. That of which he approves is fed with gold; that from which he turns the breast dies like a vagrant's child; while in and out of his voluminous skirts run a motley and monstrous progeny, a callow, a whining, a puking brood of bastard bantlings, a race of Aztecs that disgrace the intelligence of the English nation. Into this nursery none can enter except in baby clothes; and the task of discriminating between a divided skirt and a pair of trousers is performed by the librarian. Deftly his fingers lift skirt and under-skirt, and if the examination prove satisfactory the sometimes decently attired dolls are packed in tin-cornered boxes, and scattered through every drawing-room in the kingdom, to be in rocking-chairs fingered and fondled by the "young person" until she longs for some newer fashion in literary frills and furbelows. Mudie is the law we labour after; the suffrage of young women we are supposed to gain: the paradise of the English novelist is in the school-room: he is read there or nowhere. And yet it is certain that never in any age or country have writers been asked to write under such restricted conditions; if the same test by which modern writers are judged were applied to their forefathers, three-fourths of the contents of our libraries would have to be condemned as immoral publications. Now of the value of conventional innocence I don't pretend to judge, but I cannot help thinking that the cultivation of this curiosity is likely to run the nation into literary losses of some magnitude.

It will be said that genius triumphs over circumstances, but I am not sure that this is absolutely the case; and turning to Mr. Mathew Arnold, I find that he is of the same opinion. He says, . . . "but it must have the atmosphere, it must find itself in the order of ideas, to work freely, and this is not so easy to command. This is why the great creative epochs in literature are so rare . . . because for the creation of a master work of literature two powers must concur, the power of the man and the power of the moment; the creative has for its happy exercise appointed elements, and those elements are not in its own control." I agree with Mr. Mathew Arnold. Genius is a natural production, just as are chickweed and roses; under certain conditions it matures; under others it dies; and the deplorable dearth of talent among the novelists of to-day is owing to the action of the circulating library, which for the last thirty years has been staying the current of ideas, and quietly opposing the development of fresh thought. The poetry, the history, the biographies written in our time will live because they represent the best ideas of our time; but no novel written within the last ten years will live through a generation, because no writer pretends to deal with the moral and religious feeling of his day; and without that no writer will, no writer ever has been able to, invest his work with sufficient vitality to resist twenty years of criticism. When a book is bought it is read because the reader hopes to find an expression of ideas of the existence of which he is already dimly conscious.

A literature produced to meet such hopes must of necessity be at once national and pregnant with the thought of the epoch in which it is written. Books, on the contrary, that are sent by the librarian to be returned in a few days, are glanced at with indifference, at most with the vapid curiosity with which we examine the landscape of a strange country seen through a railway-carriage window. The bond of sympathy that should exist between reader and writer is broken —a bond as sacred and as intimate as that which unites the tree to the earth—and those who do not live in communion with the thought of their age are enabled to sell their characterless trash; and a writer who is well known can command as large a sale for a bad book as a good one. The struggle for existence, therefore, no longer exists; the librarian rules the roost; he crows, and every chanticleer pitches his note in the same key. He, not the ladies and gentlemen who place their names on the title-pages, is the author of modern English fiction. He models it, fashions it to suit his purpose, and the artistic individualities of his employés count for as little as that of the makers of the pill-boxes in which are sold certain well-known and mildly purgative medicines. And in accordance with his wishes English fiction now consists of either a sentimental misunderstanding, which is happily cleared up in the end, or of singular escapes over the edges of precipices, and miraculous recoveries of one or more of the senses of which the hero was deprived, until the time has come for the author to bring his tale to a close. The novel of observation, of analysis, exists no longer among us. Why? Because the librarian does not feel as safe in circulating a study of life and manners as a tale concerning a lost will.

To analyze, you must have a subject; a religious or sensual passion is as necessary to the realistic novelist as a disease to the physician. The dissection of a healthy subject would not, as a rule, prove interesting, and if the right to probe and comment on humanity's frailties be granted, what becomes of the pretty schoolroom, with its piano tinkling away at the "Maiden's Prayer," and the water-colour drawings representing mill-wheels and Welsh castles? The British mamma is determined that her daughter shall know nothing of life until she is married; at all events, that if she should learn anything, there should be no proof of her knowledge lying about the place—a book would be a proof; consequently the English novel is made so that it will fit in with the "Maiden's Prayer" and the water-mill. And as we are a thoroughly practical nation, the work is done thoroughly; root and branch are swept away, and we begin on a fresh basis, just as if Shakespeare and Ben Jonson had never existed. A novelist may say, "I do not wish to enter into those pretty schoolrooms. I agree with you, my book is not fit reading for young girls; but does this prove that I have written an immoral book?" The librarian answers, "I cater for the masses, and the masses are young unmarried women who are supposed to know but one side of life. I cannot therefore take your book." And so it comes to pass that English literature is sacrificed on the altar of Hymen.

But let me not be misunderstood. I would not have it supposed that I am of opinion that literature can be glorified in the Temples of Venus. Were the freedom of speech I ask for to lead to this, we should have done no more than to have substituted one evil for another. There is a middle course, and I think it is this—to write as grown-up men and women talk of life's passions and duties. On one hand there must be no giggling over stories whispered in the corners of rooms; on the other, there must be no mock moral squeamishness about speaking of vice. We must write as our poems, our histories, our biographies are written, and give up once and for ever asking that most silly of all silly questions, "Can my daughter of eighteen read this book?" Let us renounce the effort to reconcile those two irreconcilable things—art and young girls. That these young people should be provided with a literature suited to their age and taste, no artist will deny; all I ask is that some means may be devised by which the novelist will be allowed to describe the moral and religious feeling of his day as he perceives it to exist, and to be forced no longer to write with a view of helping parents and guardians to bring up their charges in all the traditional beliefs.

It is doubtless a terrible thing to advocate the breaking down of the thirty-one and sixpenny safeguards, and to place it in the power of a young girl to buy an immoral book if she chooses to do so; but I am afraid it cannot be helped. Important an element as she undoubtedly is in our sociological system, still we must not lose sight of everything but her; and that the nineteenth century should possess a literature characteristic of its nervous, passionate life, I hold is as desirable, and would be as far-reaching in its effects, as the biggest franchise bill ever planned. But even for the alarmed mother I have a word of consolation. For should her daughter, when our novels are sold for half-a-crown in a paper cover, become possessed of one written by a member of the school to which I have the honour to belong, I will vouch that no unfortunate results are the consequence of the reading. The close analysis of a passion has no attraction for the young girl. When she is seduced through the influence of a novel, it is by a romantic story, the action of which is laid outside the limits of her experience. A pair of lovers—such as Paul and Virginia—separated by cruel fate, whose lives are apparently nothing but a long cry of yearning and fidelity, who seem to live, as it were, independent of the struggle for life, is the book that more often than any other leads to sin; it teaches the reader to look to a false ideal, and gives her—for men have ceased to read novels in England—erroneous and superficial notions of the value of life and love.

All these evils are inherent in the "select" circulating library, but when in addition it sets up a censorship and suppresses works of which it does not approve, it is time to appeal to the public to put an end to such dictatorship, in a very practical way, by withdrawing its support from any library that refuses to supply the books it desires to read.

GEORGE MOORE.